P9-EDY-209

To Leonardo
an Karen

People I really love
and want to get
to know better —

5 Jul 96

Jay Frankston

THE GIRL
IN THE PICTURE

AND OTHER POEMS

by Jay Frankston

Cover by Bettina Lewis Sluzki

by the same author
available from
Whole Loaf Publications:

A Christmas Story, *a true tale*

Seeds, *a Collection of Sayings
and Things*

The Offering, *a Series of Meditations
on the Meaning of Life*

Copyright © 1996
by Whole Loaf Publications
All rights reserved

Some of these poems have previously
 been published in various magazines

Published by
Whole Loaf Publications
Little River, CA 95456
(707) 937-0208

e-mail wlp@mcn.org
http://www.mcn.org/a/wlp/christmas

ISBN 0-9629754-6-X
First Edition
Manufactured in the U.S.A.

to the Great Unknown
from whence much of this came

(and to the poet in each of us)

CONTENTS

ABOUT POETRY

It all started after I had attended a number of poetry readings. I write but I seldom write poetry. At the readings, which were more or less well attended, the reader emoted his poems to the audience and each poem was followed by a collective sigh. I even found myself being part of that collective sigh. But, although I enjoyed the listening, deep down inside I had to admit that I didn't know what the poem was about. I refused to acknowledge my ignorance and, like all the others, said something like "That was wonderful". But I was hungry for meaning.

Then one day, at a reading at the Kelly House in Mendocino, I felt daring. I turned to my neighbor, someone I had known for a long time, and asked her if she understood the poem. To my surprise she said she didn't. Upon asking others I found that most of them didn't understand it either, though they liked it. I was annoyed, upset, almost angry.

I remembered when, in New York City quite a number of years ago, I had been into oil painting. I wasn't a good painter, just a rank amateur. But I was into "meaningful" art and spent as much as six months on a painting that I called "The Orphans", or "The Eternal Swing", or "The Children of God". And I went to the Whitney Museum one day and looked at something entitled "White on White" or some such thing, and other canvases covered with random blotches of paint. I was annoyed, upset, almost angry then.

Coming home from this exhibit I stormed into my studio, took out a large canvas and set it on the easel. I took a 6 foot-long rag, dipped it in oil and some odd colors and, standing several feet away, I whipped the canvas with color for 15 minutes. Then I took a long stick, tied a brush at the end, and drew several lines on the canvas from afar. The whole thing took less than half an hour. A few days later, when the canvas was dry, I framed it and hung it up on my living room wall, right alongside "The Apple Pickers" and "The Children of God". I called this one "The Joke" because, to me, that's what it was.

When people came to visit they looked at the paintings on my wall and nodded. But when they came to that one, they oohed and aahed, telling me that they saw storms, and ocean waves, and mysterious mountains and what not. When I told them that it was a joke, that I had painted it in jest and anger, they nodded. "That's it" they insisted "your anger shows on the canvas and makes it come alive. It doesn't matter what your intention was.

It's a good painting because of it, not in spite of it."
I never forgot that. Still I recognized that I had
no real conception of color or perspective, and I gave
up painting.

So here I was many years later, coming
away from a poetry reading, feeling the same kind
of annoyance, anger, and rebelliousness.

When I got home, I sat in an armchair
with a pad and pencil and, in less than half an
hour, I wrote three poems, in jest or so I thought. I
then read them to my wife. When I was finished, I
heard a small sigh coming from her, a sigh not
unlike the ones I had heard at the readings. I
think I even heard one from me.

When I reread these three poems a few
days later I found myself thinking that this one was
better than that one, and that one was not as good
as the other. Wow! A value judgment. That implies
value, merit. I astounded myself.

In the next few days I wrote some 18
poems, all of them at night, all of them in spurts
over brief periods of time, and all of them without
intention or conscious thought. I don't know why,
but I liked them. Still it bothered me that I had put
so little time and effort in them, and without it I
thought they had little merit.

Then I remembered having gone to the Van Gogh Museum in Amsterdam some years ago. As I looked at the paintings I noticed the year in which they were painted. It astounded me to see the huge number that were painted in the same year. There must have been over 250 of them. Then there were sketches and what not. And I knew there were works of Van Gogh in other museums around the world. He must have completed a painting in a few hours I thought to myself in awe.

One day I spoke of this to a friend and he said something that I recall now. He said "No! Of course not! It didn't take Van Gogh a few hours to paint a canvas. It took him thirty some-odd years to get to the point where he could paint a canvas in a few hours." The meaning of what he said is clear to me now .

I guess it took me over sixty years to get to where I could spontaneously come out with a meaningful poem in a relatively brief period of time. I look at these poems and recognize events in my past woven in and out of them, subconscious thoughts and emotions which pierced through when I allowed the words to flow without filtering them. So now I write poetry without explanation or apology.

JAY FRANKSTON

PANNING
FOR GOLD

You stand in color and skin
brightly lit and wet
and glistening
with tiny pearls of sweat
like a crown upon your forehead
grains of sand washed up
against your feet
and not an ocean in sight.

You lean against a yellow thread
a dancing girl on a circus tightrope
the umbrella over your head
and a hat in the Easter Parade
on one of those Sundays on Fifth Avenue.

"Come" you said and walked away
trailing your light like a comet
like the train on the wedding dress
you never got to wear.

And you peered at me
through the slats of the venetian blind
on the window of the hotel room
where the sign kept blinking
"Vacancy", "Vacancy".

But I didn't know how to whistle.

Take an object off the floor,
pick it up, stretch it out,
lay it flat on the table,
write on it, iron it,
put it in a frame
and hang it on the wall,
use it as a picture,
a dart board, a mirror,
look at it, look into it,
see the reflection
flicker with uncertainty,
like ripples on the water,
put your hand through it,
reach in and pull out
a jelly Dali clock,
where time drips over
the edge of the canvas,
minutes, like drops on the floor,
a splash of eternity
hanging on the wall.

To be really appreciated, a poem needs to be read twice.
Once for the music. Once for the words.

Fifteen years before the flood
I was riding a bus
with my briefcase on my lap.
There were things on my mind
a paycheck in my pocket
and dreams tucked away
in my sleeve
. . .and then the phone rang.

When the meeting broke up
we all went home and watched TV,
but I left my briefcase on the bus
and it sizzled on the back burner.
There was something in it
that was very important
and it found its way into my dreams.
I was caught in a storm
the briefcase floating down the river
or falling out the window
. . . and then the phone rang.

Was it a bus or the subway?
Did I really have a briefcase?
I can't remember now.
It's all so vague.
But it was important,
very important,
just before the phone rang.

Reach in! Reach in deep
under the surface
under the skin
under the fear.
Reach in under the layers
of crust and life
through the masks, the disguises
the Halloweens of time
through the forests
of frightening fairy tales,
the tiny kernel of self
naked and vulnerable,
trembling, pulsating,
beating like a heart
sending silent messages
to the wind
sending tiny little sparks
of uniqueness
to the surface of this calloused being
making it quiver
making it dance
making it live in spite of itself
when the rest of the world
has gone numb.

Snap! It breaks.
The ice melts.
Five golden-haired ladies
dancing in a liquid cloud
of bourbon on ice
repeated many times
in a glass in a bar
where loggers jostle each other
with chain saws
whose teeth are filled
with the flesh of trees
now lying lifeless and still
in the mill yard.
Toothpicks on the counter
of the all-night diner
where the waitress with the big boobs
leans over and pours you
another cup of coffee
hinting that she gets off at midnight
when the streets are empty
and there's room for dancing.
But you can't make it tonight
and she looks disappointed
and her hair curls deeper
into her head
as you zip up your pants
bring your belly over your belt
lift the chain saw off the counter
and go home.

I heard it on the radio.
The sun was shining.
They called it a disaster, a catastrophe.
All those people.
I was in love.
And it came all at once,
no warning, no telegram,
no knock on the door.
No one believed it.
The earth trembled
and I felt myself tremble inside.
Some jumped out of windows
like during the depression
hoping that love had wings
and would carry them.

Great gushes of lava from my eyes
down the sides of my face,
the mountain, a fountain, a volcano,
an eruption down deep, deep,
deep where the water comes from.

Everyone was running,
women with babies in their arms
looking for the fathers of their children
in the streets, in the doorways,
in the confusion.

And I held on for dear life
to the only meaning I knew,
earthquakes where feelings bleed hot
and surface only by accident
on the radio.

Comes the dawn all bets are off,
the night was not for sleeping.
With windshield wipers broken,
my eyes have the color of rain.
From high above on a redwood tree
a branch snaps and falls.
In the hissing silence I am numb.
I can't even feel the pain.
I didn't know the thirteenth month
came long after my birthday.
The fire went out in the hearth
and we sat and watched it die
then March and April went by.

Many songs have I heard since then.
A tree is a tree is a tree.
But the wood splinters at the edges
and my fingers are caught in the crack.
Now the ribbon stretches before me
and twists, and turns, and whines,
and the voice of the forest whispers.
There's no place left to hide.

They're looking for you.
What have you done?
In the house with the broken window
there's a hush on the wall.
The shades are drawn in pen and ink
but the night slipped in anyway.
You must have done something.
It sits in the empty chair
in the middle of the room
and reads you dreams
from A Tale of Two Cities,
London and Paris,
the two Jerusalems.

On the other side you are absent.
Seven days and seven nights you fasted,
listening for the raven's call.
Then your alarm went off
in the middle of the night
and you left with it.
Now they're looking for you
but they'll never find you.
Joshua fought the battle of Jericho
but you're not even on the map.

It always comes up
when someone is talking
and you can never quite
make out what it is.
But it rides on the words
and circles around
and everyone else
seems to know.
So you stand in the corner
and feel left out
or pretend you can play
just like they.
The next thing you know
you've told them the truth
and they didn't want to hear it.
So they shrugged it off,
tied on a few words,
and buried it at sea.

Look where you're going,
you crazy bastard.
The street belongs to us all.
The bulls are running in Pamplona,
filling empty spaces.
But someone's got to do the laundry,
socks and jeans and pillow cases.
The ride wasn't worth the dime
so bring me back to the gate.
There's a way to enter
without being seen,
like threading a needle,
or a walk through the catacombs
the skulls looking back at you,
and winking.
The bulls are running in Pamplona,
filling empty spaces,
and you coil up like a snake,
you crazy bastard.
You don't even know your name
and look where you are now,
on a stage in the theatre.
The curtain is up
and they're all staring at you,
but you forgot your lines.
You forgot your lines
you crazy bastard.
Why don't you get off?
The bulls are running in Pamplona.

"WHAT AM I DOING YOU ASK?"

I'm panning for gold.

I ramble on in words on paper with no compass and no sense of direction, not screening the meaningless for the meaningful. A mudful of words in a sieve, looking for a phrase, perhaps a sentence, that's made out of silver, or iron, or gold, one that will brighten the sky or lighten the load, explode into stars or just make you cry. One of those rare finds that can lift you up and spin you around.

(When you're panning for gold
you sometimes get a nugget)

Zihuatanejo

It's been like a fever
under the hot sun
climbing vines
up the coconut tree
seven layers above the horizon
where ships sail
forever out of sight
never looking back
never seeing the foam in their wake
strings of pearls
hanging from their mast.
Wind in your hair
in your sails
under your fingernails
scratching out a living
among the barefoot children
and the bare-boned dogs
hoping to find an answer
to the questions of life
or just a means of living it out
without sinking under the weight
of the heat, the poverty
the dregs of uncared for homes
with dirt floors and pigs
and roosters crowing all night
to the distress of those
who try to sleep.

A nugget

Seven layers above the horizon
there are ships that sail
forever out of sight
never looking back
never seeing the foam in their wake
strings of pearls hanging from their mast

There's only the running!
Grab a fistful of dust
and hold on, hold on tight.
A balloon, like a dream
at the end of a kite.
It's all there and gone
when you open your eyes.
A heartbeat away from yesterday.

There's only the running
and those who run behind,
pushing you on,
pushing you off,
pushing you over.

The wind blows through the trees.
Another year gone by,
another candle on the cake.
Let's dance you say,
but the musicians went home,
and the lights are out,
and there are no butterflies at night.

Now there's only the running
and I forget where,
and I forget why.
No place to go.
No place to stop.

The fist is clenched
and there's nothing in it,
nothing but the moment
when now breaks open into forever.
Then who will look after the baby?

A nugget

There is no time.
There's only the moment
when now breaks open
into forever

In the middle of the ocean,
in the middle of life,
there's an island somewhere.
Shipwrecked souls
find their way to its shore
and drink from coconuts
the milk of sight.
And the visions guide them
through fires and storms,
to a state of being
they never knew before.

In the middle of the middle
there's a tiny hole
through which life escapes
when no one's looking,
and the flower pot with the wilted flower
falls from the window sill
unto the street below.
It crashes on the sidewalk
but no one hears it.

They're all asleep somewhere
in classrooms, in concert halls,
on park benches
with newspapers over their heads
to shade them from the light of the world,
from a bland reality
where there are no stones,
no broken glass,
no angry voices,
just the waves of the ocean
crashing on a beach,
on some far away island
in the middle of life

Standing on the head of a pin,
listening at the keyhole of eternity,
hoping to hear it speak, to me,
of time which it knows not,
in words which it knows not,
about birth and death
and stagnation.

Standing at the window of my life,
watching the children
play in the fields,
their hair tousled
careless and free,
watching the bees suckle honey
from the flowers,
watching the deer looking up,
watching me,
waiting for the bus, for the train,
for the phone to ring,
as time passes,
and the wind blows,
and the birds fly south for the winter.

Standing on the edge of forever
reaching in for a handful of nows.

It was caught in a breath of thin air.
I lost sight of it
when it fluttered against the sun
and vanished in the light.
But it flutters still,
rising and falling
in my chest, in my heart,
in the darkroom of my mind
where all the prints are made
from the same negative
and blown out of all proportion
to accommodate those who are blind,
or nearsighted, or just plain stupid.
It's always a difficult ride
in the tunnel of horrors
where your past jumps out at you
and claws at your mother,
your father, your brother,
or just falls flat on its face.

A nugget

There is a darkroom in your mind
where all the prints are made
from the same negative,
and blown out of all proportion

Picture postcards
speaking loudly in sepia brown
of other times, not long ago.
The Charleston and flappers in furs,
fingers crossed on a roll of the dice
at the crap table in Vegas,
in Reno, in Monte Carlo,
rubbing shoulders with high society,
rubbing elbows with the rich and famous,
rubbing the grime off the dirty bathtub
to give the baby a bath.

Picture postcards
from strange places
behind the mind's eye,
with no destination
and no point of origin,
like bottles in the ocean
or empty beer cans
all along the freeway,
tossed to the wind
from passing cars,
the only thing that escapes
from the moving vehicle
other than the exhaust.

Picture postcards
under the magnet
on the refrigerator,
reminders of places
never been and yet to go,
rays of light coming from windows
that exist only in the imagination
but breathe life into the dreary present.

The forgotten dream

With eyes half open
and sleep still hugging my body
I wake unto this paper
to hold on to the dream.
But the thread is broken.
The dream is gone.
It dissolved behind my reaching.
Still it ripples through me
and through my day,
filtering the flow.
And I stand, and I move
with a slight trembling motion
the dream still taking up space.
I know it is there
like a leaf on my shoulder.
And I walk quietly
so as not to disturb it.

A man speaks to himself
and the dog listens.
There are no blunders
in a night flight.
The calendar is tacked on the wall
pinned like a butterfly
to remind us
of birthdays we've missed
because there was no mail that day
or someone had died
and it didn't matter.
You work too hard
you drink too much
and the genie is still in the lamp.
There are ripe berries
on magic bushes
and a tree out there
you haven't climbed yet.
That's the way it is.
There is no changing it.
The clock repeats 6 o'clock
twice every day.
But somewhere in the world
a man speaks to himself
and the dog listens
and understands.

A nugget

You work too hard.
You drink too much
and the genie is still in the lamp.
There are ripe berries
on magic bushes
and a tree out there
you haven't climbed yet.

They'll take your soul if you let them.
Your picture in their photo album
gathering dust over the years
flattened between the pages
of their forgetfulness
and the occasional question:
"Who was that person anyway?"
Or maybe confusing you
for someone else's cousin
the one who fell in love with Helen,
or was it Zeus?
Who remembers? Who cares?
Who has a soul anyway?
They can't take what you don't have.
I traded mine long ago
to a travelling merchant
and he left me with a question
to which I don't have the answer
and it itches in my clothes
and aches in my head
and pounds in my chest.
So go ahead!
Take my picture!
I don't care.
You won't get my soul
in that photograph.

A nugget

They've got your picture
in their photo album
gathering dust over the years,
flattened between the pages
of their forgetfulness
and the occasional question:
"Who was that person anyway?"

Crisp breaking night
opens on a bed of flowers
wrinkled with age.
Petals, like fingers
like tongues, like algae
on the bottom of the ocean
reaching up for the light
through fish-laden water
which sways, and ebbs and flows
and throws itself splashing
white foam on a beach
leveling the sand castle
of yesterday's child
now grown older
now a man
whose only castles are in the air
the crisp night air
of unbroken silence.

It doesn't matter where you go
or even where you come from,
the tree grows in one direction,
roots in the ground like a siphon
sucking up life
and expanding out
through the trunk,
the branches, the leaves,
making a canopy of shade
under which you stand
a stranger, a wanderer,
on your way from nowhere to nowhere,
resting there for a moment
to slow the momentum
to look at the map,
regroup, and let the engine cool.
To feel the mass of the tree
the strength of forever
the wisdom of patience.
Just waiting in silence
for things to come
without going out to get them.

Above the mantelpiece of ignorance
hangs the portrait
of someone who wasn't born yet.
He lies in wait
for generations to come
to lay a wreath
upon the tomb
of the unknown soldier,
purple heart, silver star,
four times decorated
in 3 successive wars
a heavy price to pay
for stealing the apple
of Adam's tree.

The scream

Write your name on the wall
pin it up on the bulletin board
under the magnet of the refrigerator
or make it graffiti
on the New York subway.
Tell them who you are
make it loud so they'll hear
voices screaming in the night
shouting at the moon
at the stars
I am here! I am here!
The shout into a whisper
and the waves erasing
its mark on the sand.
And I, I alone on a park bench
feeding the pigeons
and waiting for a handout
from the stranger who passes by
and doesn't know me
and doesn't know himself
and walks on
looking for a wall
to write his name upon.

First day of Spring
a celebration for those
who are still counting
the days in a month
the seasons in a year
the birthdays that are better
left uncounted
reminders of winters past
and winters to come
reminders that today
must be a celebration
no matter what
no matter when
and drinking in the day
with thirst and gusto
to fill the empty holding tanks
on the water towers of our lives
for a time when it stops raining
and the drought sets in
or the city doesn't deliver the water.
So you can take it up where you left off
and resume counting the days
till summer, till winter
till the next first day of Spring.

A nugget

Drink in the day
with thirst and gusto
to fill the empty holding tanks
on the water towers of your life

THE CURSE OF THE POET

The musician walks down the street carrying his guitar case and everyone he passes nods and smiles. They acknowledge his music and ask him to play. It doesn't matter that they've heard his song before. They'll hear it again. They won't wait for him to pull out his guitar. They'll ASK him for his music and thank him for the gift.

And here is the poet walking down the street with fresh new poems in his notebook, like crisp iceberg lettuce, and everyone inquires about his health, his garden, his plans for the summer, but no one asks "Have you written anything lately?" or "Would you read us one of your poems."

Once in a while he corners somebody, like in the cartoon of the man in the isle of the airplane with a gun in his hand, and all the frightened passengers with their hands up and the man says:

"DON'T WORRY EVERYONE. NOTHING IS GOING TO HAPPEN. I JUST WANTED YOU TO HEAR MY POEM."

And maybe he gets to read a poem or two once, maybe twice and that's it. It's the end, the poem is spent. That's all the life it has. It's not much more than a stamp on an envelope. One mailing and it's cancelled, obliterated. It sinks into oblivion.

And the wretched poet walks on, with mouth gagged, and poems stuffed in his back pocket, jumping around like jumping beans, seeking to breathe the air, but stifled like a sneeze you hold on to, or a cough no one wants to hear.

Sanctuary

Sixteen weeks on a merry-go-round
gives you a hell of a spin.
I see them running, tripping, falling,
priests in white robes, on holy ground,
looking for God under a desert tent,
barefoot children, old men on crutches,
women screaming, wailing, weeping,
trying to get to the other side,
over the wall, the fence, the barbed wire,
feeling the eye, like a bee on your shoulder,
about to strike, to bite, to sting,
crawling through the sewers
under the city,
with the stars so close
you can feel them in your hair,
floodlights combing the night for rats,
moving in fear across the bridge,
the river, the sea, carrying words
and loaves of unleavened bread.

The men, on horses,
nostrils flaring,
giant hooves on buttercups.

Don't look back, it's only yesterday.
There is no time.
The earth breaks open under our feet
"Sanctuary! Sanctuary!"

When the walls are thin
you can hear the bed heaving
under the sex-laden mattress,
you can hear the neighbors arguing
in violet liquor tones
while the baby cries hysterically
in his cardboard crib.

When the walls are thin
you can feel the hunger of children
in Somalia, or Bosnia
or the ghettoes of L.A.
Broken bones around the hearth
and a cold wind under the door.

When the walls are thin
everyone's problems
become your own
a large wooden cross
over the bed
and a statue of Mary
on the night table.
You must learn to swim
or you drown.

When the walls are thin
you'd better be quiet
or the neighbors will hear you
writing your poetry
in the middle of the night.

Rooms for rent
by the day
by the hour
in sleazy hotels
where condoms are provided
but you bring your own whore.
Streets lit up
with walking cigarettes
in high-heel shoes
and fishnet stockings.
Invitations whispered
in dollars and cents.
Stark offers of sex on rye
for here or to go.
Dark alleys
where drugs are played
like a crap game.
Anyone can play
but no one wins.
The cat's in the cradle
or the garbage can.
The graffiti on the wall
screams desperately
to those who walk by
without seeing.
And the sky turns grey
and hides in a blanket of clouds.

Great Scott!
The time is running.
The track is wet.
There are no signals.
We live in Disneyland.
Mountains of garbage
sliding down on us
like lava from the volcano
of our greed.
Spoiled adults
feeding children
the leftovers
from their forty years feast.
"I'm not hungry Mom.
Leave me an acre
of pristine earth
and I can plant my future
where you buried your past."
What will we do when the rains come
and wash us all away?

"Taxi!"

It begins with a tickle
in someone's groin
and it tap dances
on the roof of his yellow Pontiac
as she sits beside him,
a passenger.

It turns into a sigh
at the end of her breath
as she looks at his picture
with the number beneath it
inmate of some wife
he divorced many years ago.

It comes in through the window
and mixes with the noise of the traffic
when he speaks in broken English.
Luis Ramon, 46 years old.
He's not even good-looking
but he knows his way around.

It breaks into a fancy
in her glove and her shoe
and the wild wind of her imagination
as she sees him in profile
against the background
of her sexual fantasy.

"Pull over, driver,
I think I'll sit in back."

Breathe in the crimson sun
heaven rides on iron wheels
much has gone from city streets
paved hopes and potted dreams
studded belts and leather jackets.

Society's child is an orphan.

Breathe out through eyes of steel
bright headlights on armored cars
a two-dollar bill and some pocket change
the weeds grow in your shadow.

Sorrow sleeps in empty drawers.

Breathe in the watered garden
splintered thoughts made whole again
trees so ancient the mind barely remembers
but the heart beats strong
and the river flows
where thirsty men crouch down.

Breathe out the sense of loss
no schedules to follow
no time tables to read
wild geese flap their wings
and the nest is empty of swallows.

A footnote in yesterday's paper.

In the dream where cheap wine flows
there are bright lights
and dance-hall girls
red-winged birds that fly free
and swallows that return
from the bottle
and explode into light
warming the blood
making the eyes sparkle
for a moment
and the lip curl up.

There are beds for 25 cents
the price of admission
smoke-filled rooms
wild horses on the Pampa
and men curled up in the fetus position
in doorways that are heated.

You can see through a haze
cotton eyes in the window
the reflection of someone younger
someone wiser
someone who can tie his shoelaces
and ride a bicycle.

In the dream where cheap wine flows
days blend into nights.
Time runs like urine against the wall
and people have stopped caring.

Blow me away!
Everything is changing.
Millions of years
squeezed into
a fast-paced minute.
Soon it will all fade
in a flash of lightning
and bright-colored candles
on a child's birthday cake
will be the only light left
when the world turns dark.

How do you pour the wine
that flows on vintage
and rains on you
like a sacrament?

How do you play the poverty game
when the stakes are children
and hell has a seat
on the sidewalk?

How do you spell the word
that has no meaning
when the cup is empty
and the door is locked?

How do you feed the baby
when the milk is dry
and everyone's watching
the ball game?

Break the pattern.
Let it go.
Open the pores
of the mind.
Rivers flow
deep inside
uncontrollable.
Spontaneous eruptions
of the volcano
that belches
hot lava of words
running down the white paper
making it glow
making it burn
the hand
and wake
the mind
to return it to the helm
restore control
and bring life back
to the predictable.

She takes the seeds from her womb,
scatters them to the wind
and sings to them, the Mother.
And the wind lifts them high
above fields, above fears,
takes them round and round
then lets them fall.
And flowers and trees
and children grow from the earth.
And the sun shines upon them
and makes them blossom.
And time watches,
counts, and waits for them.

Around the corner
the panhandler stands
with his hand stretched out:
"Spare any change, Mister?"
There's Vietnam in his head,
and the blades of the helicopter
keep roaring in his ears.
And the children duck
at unexpected times
as if they could hear them too.
But it's another war they hear,
the one that follows
the one that's ahead.
And they know, the children, they know
that it will take them and bleed them
and drop them from the sky.
And the Mother will scoop them up
and return them to her womb
and refuse to give birth again.

There are dreams
in which you can hide,
that bob up and down on the water
like bait at the end of the line.
Hotel Terminus it's called
but it doesn't end there,
it continues.

There are dreams that
burn, baby, burn
in cradles of hope,
where the neighborhood playground
is more than a slide into the gutter
or a seesaw that goes up and down
and nothing changes.

There are dreams
that lay on pillows,
like butterflies or buttercups.
The thread is pulled
through the eye of the needle
and comes out on the other side.

You've been there
but that's not you
eating the leftovers
on the tables at McDonald's.

THE GIRL
IN THE PICTURE

When the wind blows
the girl in the picture
opens her umbrella
and takes off her shoes.
The leaves rustle
and dance around her
as she twirls with them
and rises above the ground.
Her dreams come alive
in purple, yellow, and green,
and wild geese flap their wings
alongside of her.
And she whispers to the wind
holds up the golden slipper
and giggles under her breath.
Next to the tree
a small dog looks up,
wags its tail and barks.
Then the wind stops abruptly,
leaving her hanging in midair.
And the girl in the picture
closes the umbrella,
puts on her shoes
and watches her dreams
flutter to the ground.

I went to bed
turned off the light
slipped into the envelope
and mailed myself to sleep.
The postage stamp
was a collector's item
from an album
in some musty old attic.
And I landed there
in a trunk full of hats,
and granny clothes,
tux and tails that I tried on
to go to the formal
ball of my dreams.

Have you ever been
where God meets King
and the piper plays a tune
upon man's lips?
Has the Little Prince
landed on your planet
and gone hunting for butterflies
or chasing rainbows?
Can you look in the mirror
and laugh at yourself
even if the mirror is broken?
Is there a red balloon
on a string somewhere
looking for your finger?
Can you come back to earth
having lived on the sun
and still remember how to swim?
Will the stranger at your door
thinking you're not home walk away
without ringing the doorbell?
Is there a light in your window
like a lighthouse in the sky
to remind passersby
they are lost at sea?
Will Dennis the Menace
take Garfield to Doonesbury
and invite Charlie Brown to the dance?
And can we drink to the future
and live in the past
while the circus is in town?

At the end of the street
where the dog barks
under the street lamp
the man with the torn coat
digs through the garbage can
to find a rainbow
that will take him fishing for trout
in the rivers of his childhood.

At the end of the rainbow
there's a man with a torn coat
leaning against a street lamp,
watching a dog
dig through the garbage can
to find the bone he had buried
under a tree somewhere, long ago.

At the end of somewhere
there's a man in a rainbow
digging under a street lamp
to find the torn coat
that he can put around the dog
he found yelping in the garbage can
before taking him home.

I'd like to invite you into my poem.
Please take off your shoes!
There are lines on both sides,
a rhyme and a riddle,
and a door at the end of the hall.
In each of the rooms
the guests are asleep,
the soldier in the arms of his war,
the farmer snores next to his cow,
and the customer next to his whore.
There's a man in pajamas
heading for the bathroom,
the poet is barefoot and sleepwalking.
This happens a lot
and when the moon is full
he sometimes walks on the walls.
Then forgotten words fall out of his pockets
and arrange themselves into a poem.

I'm the person who loves you

I've picked you up and brought you down
and patted you on the back
I've made you run till you're out of breath
and ignored you when you were sad.

No! I'm not your friend.
I'm the person who loves you.

You cannot shelter in my arms
or suck my teat or call my name.
I cannot even comfort you
by holding you or scolding you.

No! I'm not your mother.
I'm the person who loves you.

I have no name, no face, no body.
You cannot touch my hair or hold my hand.
I stir your heart and awaken your soul.

No! I'm not your lover.
I'm the person who loves you

. . . in the dream.

It's apple sauce!

"All I really need to know
I learned in kindergarten."

When you are with a child
you have an excuse . . .
to get on a swing or a seesaw
to go to the zoo or the circus
to act silly, make faces, look at cartoons,
and lick the ice cream off your fingers
to hug and kiss without reason
even people you don't know very well,
to sing simple songs
play Simon says
drink hot chocolate or suck on a lollipop,
to go to birthday parties
and wear birthday hats
you have an excuse . . .
to play with crayons and draw
even if you have no talent at all
to read fairy tales to yourself
and take naps in the afternoon
after Sesame Street, Mister Rogers,
and Looney Tunes,

. . . .

. . . .

to play croquet,
make mud pies,
build tree houses
or castles in the sand,
to hug stuffed animals,
like teddy bears, or unicorns,
or soft fluffy elephants,
and learn once again
what it's like to be five
or six or seven.
It's apple sauce!

But you're an adult now
and you're not allowed to pretend.
There are no children around
and you have no excuse.

So have a couple of drinks
or smoke that joint
not so much to loosen up
the frozen joints of your life
but to have an excuse . . .

That's alright.
It's all apple sauce!

It sits and stands
and laughs and dances
and wraps itself
around my finger.
And the spool unwinds
and pours itself out
splashing pictures
on the ground.

It gets into my hair
and makes them into dreadlocks
and pours Jamaican music
into my shoes.

It pushes and tickles
and shoves me around
and switches my shirts,
my ties, my socks,
and plays games with me
of which I don't know the rules.

It walks and flies
and gets in my eyes
and gives me visions
of yellow corn fields
and a ladybug waiting
on the tip of my finger.
A single drop of dew,

. . . .

. . . .

glistens on each blade of grass
and the sun licks it off
and smiles.

It runs and hides
and calls from far away dreams
so many years ago
when the circus was in town
and the mime with the sad eyes
offered it to me like a rose
which vanished when I reached for it.

It chuckles and claps
and horses around
turning my life into a rumpus room
and nothing I can say
can make it go away.

There are days when the wind
lays down for the sun
and children make children
of us all.

When the children heard the fiddler
they came running out of the woods
carrying music, dancing shoes, and kites.
The tune had rings and hoops and la-las
and wrapped itself around their waist.

They formed a circle round and danced.
They jumped, and clapped, and twirled.
Then the earth shook three times
and the clothes fell off their backs.

Was it a grape or a fig leaf
Adam and Eve wore?
Was guilt and shame their garment?

The children laughed.
They had no questions.

Whenever it is night
and I'm alone and lonely
I turn inward
to you my unknown friend.
You from within
and I from without
we lead such different lives.
I reach, I strive,
I struggle, I try.
You sit Za Zen
on quiet pillows.
I twist, and turn,
and sweat, and cry.
You watch me in my turmoil.
You, always being yourself.
I, always becoming.
I listen for your silent song
but my life is too loud
and your voice remains a hum
in the backroom of my mind
so I forget you often times.

COUNTING

I said ten o'clock
it's a minute past ten.
Don't you know ten o'clock
will not come back again.

A minute too soon
a minute too late
The one in between
is the minute of fate.

You thought that you had
sixty seconds to spare
Your life was determined
and you were not there.

Grow up they told me.
Grow up they said,
but they didn't leave much room.
I played hide and seek
between their dos and their don'ts
and the pants were too tight.

Get a job they said
while the weeds grew
through a crack in the sidewalk.
Somehow I knew better.
Wild women don't sing the blues.
There's a tree out there
I haven't climbed yet.

I count. I count one, I count two.
I count a lot, I count often.
As a child I counted the fingers on my hand
and the hands on the clock
and the clocks in my house
and there were many,
because time was important
my father told me.
Ten little, nine little,
eight little Indians
and 99 bottles of beer on the wall.

Later, I counted the houses on my block
in New York's Washington Heights
and the movie houses in my neighborhood.
I counted the hours I spent in them
with the coming attractions, the newsreel,
the double feature, the cartoon,
and the weekly episode of Tarzan
or Zorro or Superman.
I counted the hours I spent in the dark,
alone, fantasizing.
I counted the girls

. . . .

. . . .

I would have wanted to kiss and didn't
and the circles I made around them
before getting up the nerve
to ask one to dance.
I counted the number of times
I masturbated in one week
and worried that it might do me in,
in some way.
One, two, three strikes you're out,
the fifty states on license plates,
the Ten Commandments,
and the first ten amendments.

Then I went to college
and counted the subway stations
on the A train
between Washington Heights
and N.Y.U. Washington Square.
How many flavors of ice cream?
I counted the Saturday nights
I spent with my friends
walking up on Broadway from 42nd street,
43rd, 44th, 45th street to 72nd street
looking to pick up one, two, three girls,

. . . .

. . . .

or at least pretending.
Then I met her and we counted together
and had two children
and counted their teeth as they came out.
Now I count the years we've been married
the beds we've made love in
and the telephone poles
out the window of the train.

I count the breaths I take
before falling asleep,
the time that's gone by,
the books I've read,
the lovers I've had
and I try to remember their names.
I count the days,
the steps in a mile,
the miles in a minute,
the minutes in a year
and the number of years in my life.
I count the number of lives I've led
and will I soon stop counting.

I sit by the open window
with curtain drawn
and watch my life walk by
on the street below.

It comes early
dressed in a white suit and tie
and the aspirations of youth
drunk on Pepsi-Cola
the me-generation
Thomas Wolfe and Andy Warhol.

It rushes by under my window
carrying an umbrella
the New York Times
a schoolboy's lunch box
a wallet with $18 in it
and a picture of the me
I've never met.

At night it waits
under my lamp-post
with a book of Tennyson's poems
gold-leafed and leather-bound
and held in hand
as one might hold a bible.

And it looks up at me
once in a while
and beckons me to come down
and join the fray.
But I climb into bed
and cover my head
and hide in the folds of my dreams.

Hey Charlie!
There's a nail in the wall
in the room
with the single light bulb.
Do you remember?
Three flights up and a fire escape
but no one ever gets away.
Torn sheets on the bed
and a packed suitcase in the corner.
Stranger things have happened,
I know!
Most of the time I was there,
looking for my hat, my coat, my mother.
She laughed.
I told her and she laughed.
You never show your face at the window.
Someone might see.
Someone might tell.
Broken plaster on the ceiling.
When was it they came?
I was on the roof Charlie
Where were you?
Down in the basement,
next to the boiler room.
Oh! God! Why did you do it?

. . . .

. . . .

The key.
You gave it to them
when you opened the door.
Now there's a nail in the wall
in the empty room
and the outline of a picture
that once hung there.
That's all that's left.
Remember the face Charlie?
The smile, the eyes?
It hangs like a loose chandelier
over your head.
It was long ago I know,
But it's so hard to forget.

Get off my life!
You're crowding me
your fears, your tears, your insecurity,
wrapped up like flies in a spider web,
hang on my clothes line.
And you pretend and stand on end
and flap your wings,
like the blades of a helicopter,
and we all get out of your way.
But you reach for me
and I feel used, abused, confused.
And there you are again,
washing your face in the kitchen sink
and blowing soap bubbles in the air.

Get off my life!
It's been too long
since I've felt my own breath.
Cold sheets appeal to me.
I always pray alone.
There's so much room in your wake
I could swim the English Channel.
I could know who I am
and never have to look in the mirror.
Now I hide my dreams in my pillowcase
and I leave the windows open.
And there you are again,
raining on my garden,
feeding my pigs,
and looking like the girl
in the picture magazine.

. . . .

. . . .

Get off my life!
Your shoes are dirty.
Heavy rains below the belt.
I bend and break and mend and wake
and there you are again
shining the apple
holding the glass
brushing your hair
shaking your ass
looking disinterested
and all the time
smelling like fresh coffee
early in the morning.

Most of the time I was sitting alone
on the floor, by the bed, with soldiers of lead,
an arm torn off here, a leg missing there,
all victims of the great wars of my childhood.

The sun filtering through the window
and the shadow of the curtain,
like lightning without thunder,
brought life to my silent battlefield.

Outside, on the street,
young school mates of mine,
waiting and chanting,
sticking needles in my name,
like pins in a voodoo doll,
"Frankenstein, Frankenstein,
come on out now Frankenstein"

But I fought my battles with soldiers of lead,
alone in my room, on the floor by the bed,
charging up the hill,
bugles blowing, flags flying,
and the pain of fear inside.

When my mother came home
I ran to her arms and trembled.
She held me and smiled
but never asked why.
I didn't tell her
I was wounded that day,
and she never knew I had cried.

Tear the truth out of me
for I know it is there
deep down inside
under the skin
under the flesh
in the marrow of my bones
in the marrow of my soul.

Tear the truth out of me
for it hurts
I feel it thrashing back and forth
clawing me from within
making my life a battlefield
with everything
and everyone.

Tear the truth out of me
that I may see it
separate and apart from me
that I may judge it and decide
to deny or reject it
or swallow it again
whole and incomprehensible
but a light to shine
from an otherwise meaningless life.

I laughed when they asked me.
I didn't know it hadn't rained for years.
They were all waiting for me
when I came through the door
and I hadn't brought any.
I was the source and the source was dry.
But somehow my blood
didn't seem to coagulate.
It was all moving so fast
my head was spinning.
Soon they'd come for me
and all I could think of
was the playground of my childhood in Paris
where life was hell
but painted itself into nostalgia.
I heard the siren through the fog in my head
and we all ran into the bomb shelter
and huddled afraid, together.
But here I was alone,
stretched out in the ambulance,
a lifetime later,
red lights flashing all around,
flashbulbs going off in my head
and the interviewer asking me
something I couldn't quite make out,
something about what I had come to do
in the first place.
And all I could do is laugh.

GET A JOB!

Get a job!
don't just hang around and write
or paint, or sculpt
don't write that symphony
that poem, that novel
Get a REAL job!
One that will make you sweat
and leather-wear your skin.
One that will put calluses on your hands
cause bleeding ulcers and stress.
Get a job that pays
and pays well.
You don't have to like what you do.
If you do, then it's not
a REAL job.
Don't just hang around the house
making the beds
feeding the children
shopping for food
doing the laundry.
Do something!
Get a REAL job!
One that you can worry about
that will have overtime
with pay raises and pensions
at the end of the line
something you can retire from
if you aren't fired before then.
Be like the rest of us.
GET A REAL JOB!

WASP

White   immigrants
Anglo-Saxon   aliens
Protestant   illegals
American   one and all
Indian   clustered in barrios
Native   in the ghettos
land   of Watts
of liberty   of Warsaw
bell   riots in the streets
ringing   of Chicago
in our ears   of New Jersey
in our heads   of Harlem
in the distance   anger and frustration
in the night   exploding
by the dawn's early light   protesting
there are screams   White
in the mouths of babes   Anglo-Saxon
born Black   Protestant
Asian   dominance
Hispanic   ignorance

. . . arrogance.

Written at the time
of the Persian Gulf War

Hitch a ride to the front line
on a jeep, a tank, a troop carrier
bring your sun glasses and your camera
your fear, your adrenaline
your congressional medal of honor
C-rations, Q-tips, band aids
blood plasma, double-strength aspirin
and a joint, yes bring a joint
an exocet missile
and several rounds of ammunition
some letters from home
preferably with pictures
a message from Garcia
an "I'm proud of you son"
with a handshake from the President
the commander-in-chief
bring a six-pack of beer
a Penthouse magazine
and the score of the football game
bring a telegram from the war department
with a "We regret to inform you. . ."
bring a monument, a war memorial
and a ticker-tape parade down Broadway
bring shoe polish, a gas mask
and a high-school diploma
bring words of encouragement
from the folks back home
at the Pentagon, at the war factory

. . . .

. . . .

at the movies or the local bar
tell them I'm doing a job for my country
I'm a good American, a patriot
bring a laxative, underarm deodorant
penicillin, and the guys from M.A.S.H.
bring a prayer from someone
who still believes in God
shoe polish, bring shoe polish
Oh! I said that already
"Gee Mom. I'd like to go home"
bring Bob Hope. No! Never mind!
don't bring Bob Hope
bring nostalgia and the girls
from the Stage Door Canteen
an American flag,
yes bring an American flag, a big one
like the one we raised on Iwo Jima
bring an artificial limb or two
just in case, you know
just in case
bring a return ticket
if they aren't all sold out
and bring a where the hell am I
and what the hell am I doing here?
and something, please bring something
that will stop me from shaking.

Yesterday's hero

I was 12 years old
when I got my first axe.
Fifteen when I got my first chain saw.
I was young, and strong, and proud.
My father took me into the woods with him
and showed me how
we could tumble those giant trees,
lash them to ropes and load them into trucks
driven by men who, like us, were pioneers
in the remaining wilderness
of the pacific northwest.
Axes would swing and chips would fly
and chain saws would buzz loud and long
under the tall canopy of leaves
a hundred and fifty feet overhead.
The noise was interrupted now and then
by the shout of "TIMBER",
the cracking of the trunk
at the base of the giant,
the whistling of the fall,
and the massive thump
as it hit the ground,
the reward of long hours of hard work.
This was followed by a hollow silence
throughout the forest
before the resumption of intense activity.
We were men then. Real men!
I was strong as an ox,

. . . .

. . . .

my skin was tight and red as all outdoors
and no one asked me my age
when I ordered a beer.
I was part of the crew, a woodsman,
a lumberjack right out of the movies of the 50s
respected, admired, a hero of sorts.

Then someone went into the forest
and counted the remaining trees
and everything changed.
What was good became bad.
The hero became a villain
and everything turned upside down.
I never grew to understand it, and if I did,
I couldn't deal with it.
My life had leaned too far in one direction
to be felled in another.

I am much older now
and I drive a logging truck.
I no longer stick my head out of the cab
and smile proudly at my cargo.
I try to protect myself
behind rolled up windows
from the curses of people
who curse under their breath
as they see me drive by with, they say,
a litter of dead trees on the back

. . . .

. . . .

What I was made to be proud of
I am now made to be ashamed of.
And the medal I won
for bravery in action during the war
remains in its box at the bottom of the drawer.
It is no longer the measure
of my worth as a man.

And I feel as though my life is for naught.
I have been used.
And now, toward the end of it,
no one is there to acknowledge
the houses that have been built
with the lumber from those trees I felled
when I was young, strong, and a hero.

Speak up!
Break the silence.
Don't let them do it
without you.
There is no virtue
in acquiescence.
You're either a mover
or a silent victim.
Chain saws are buzzing.
Stars are exploding.
The rain tastes like vinegar
and oranges glow in the dark.
Speak up!
Is this your doing?
Can life go through the sieve
and come out clean?
Must we endure toxic waste
in our haste
to turn tomorrow
into yesterday?
Can we suffer our children
to survive our abuses?
Speak up!
There is no time.
Break the silence
before the dirt
falls on your face.

WORDS

BULL'S EYE

What word is this
that hangs from the lip like a spider,
silently stretching its infinity?
Tiny footsteps behind closed doors
where lovers hide from each other
and drink from empty glasses
things yet unspoken.

What word is this
in the empty envelope,
mailed without a stamp
from some never-never land,
island of childhood
where hope was a ship
on the distant horizon,
waiving handkerchiefs at passing trains
and remembering to be home by seven?

What word is this?
Sounds that escape from hollow caves
where wolves no longer bed down.
Wild dreams of boars
that run across the mind
trampling the flowers
of our long forgotten past
and the tears sting like darts
on the board marked "BULL'S EYE".

Words, words,
hanging from the clothesline
like sheets, like towels,
like pillowcases,
hanging outside, out there,
in the rain,
dripping, dripping,
dripping from the line,
from the sentence, from the meaning,
dripping from the mouth
onto the floor, the shirt, the paper,
making stains that cannot be removed.
Words without definition,
like dribble, like courage,
tiny and insignificant,
seeking attention,
splitting hairs,
splitting headaches,
splitting sentences,
falling to the ground
like dead leaves
crushed underfoot,
crumbled into dust
and blown away, away,
away into silence.

There are words that tremble
on the lips of old people
and recall a past we did not know.
There are words that stick in your throat
and words that roll off your tongue.
There are words that shout,
that sing, that play
words that lie, words of clay,
meaningless words,
that flatter, or offend,
insult, or pretend,
words without definition,
words that are foreign,
words that hold out a promise
like a politician on election day,
words that are whispered, words that pray,
words only a mother can say,
words that fit into crossword puzzles
in French, or Italian, or Greek,
words that speak,
a hundred thousand words,
like the keys on a celestial piano
endless phrases that go on and on,
words that limit, that imprison, that define,
like "No!" like "Don't!" like "Never!",
words that are clever, cuss words
that break through anger and frustration,
words you look up in the dictionary
when you are thirteen
and you can't ask anyone,
like coitus, or vagina, or copulation,
that float by in your imagination,

. . . .

. . . .

words that only lawyers use,
like Know all Men by these presents,
party of the first part,
being of sound mind, in witness whereof,
words that are vague,
ethereal words like love,
or meaning, or God,
words that escape from your mouth,
sorry words you can't take back,
that hurt like a slap in the face,
or a kick in the groin,
words that color your life like a canvas,
harsh words, green words,
ever loving mean words,
words of sorrow, words of grief,
words that are left wanting,
that echo in your mind
but won't come out when you need them,
that stutter or lisp
and have no future,
words that sound better
when they are written
than when they are spoken,
that make fun of you,
and your braces, or your glasses,
or the pimples on your face,
that bite, and sting,
like vinegar, like acid,
bloated words, pregnant words,
that give birth to love, or hate, or laughter,
and sometimes to poems like this.

Take a word, a single word,
round and smooth
like a note on the scale
like your mother's breast
or the paper weight on your father's desk
roll it on the ground
like a marble
kick it like a tin can
on the way to school
when the pimples on your face
were like pimples on your soul
put it in your pocket and feel it
between the fingers of your hand
squeeze it, count it
Spell it:

                L O V E - Me!

Take a word, a single word,
long and sharp
like a sword, like a needle
piercing, like a scream
like lightning
like a nightmare in a fisted hand
throw it like a javelin
at a distant target
run in front of it
and let it go through you.
Swallow it whole, the word:

                G O D - Me!

There are words that jump around
like crickets or frogs
and refuse to be caught
but they "ribbet".

Poet!

with your words sticking out
tied in knots, in ribbons,
wrapped around your mother,
your father, your lover,
with your words

loud, raw, naked
shouting ME all over the page
threadbare and glistening
over the white canvas

with your words
dyed in wool, dark, dim,
obscure, chasing a mood,
a rainbow, a vision,
a past better left forgotten

with your words pounding,
resounding, expounding,
sliding home between the pages
unread, words like lead,
sinking into the subconscious
making waves or only ripples
on the ear, on the air,
on the psyche.

Nobody's listening!

CELEBRATING MY SELF
IN CONTEMPLATION OF DEATH

"Died in Venice"
On the Piazza San Marco
surrounded by pigeons without wings
while the bells rang all around
and the Gondoliers dressed in black
steered flower-covered gondolas
through the canals
under the Bridge of Sighs
where I, so high,
died in Venice.

"Died in Paris"
Street urchins sailing
paper boats in the gutter
the Seine carrying the body
floating face down in the water.
the Eiffel Tower rising
like a huge phallus
from between the legs
of the Arch of Triumph
under which burns
the perpetual flame
of the unknown soldier.

"Died in Geneva"
riding a horse that threw me
while playing a game
of justice and injustice,
caught in my ideals,
victim of my compulsion
to juggle emotions
and fight windmills.

. . . .

. . . .

"Died in Budapest"
a hole in someone else's past
through which I fell,
trying to reach for the hand,
the memory of she who is long gone,
dragged down into the hell
of the ghettoes, the camps,
the ashes of loved ones
I never knew, who didn't
die in Budapest
but elsewhere.

"Died in Madrid"
at the hands of Basque anarchists
who took me for a gunrunner
while I was trying to change the tire
on the car I had rented from Avis.
"Died in Madrid"
of a heart attack
on the horns of a bull
who saw my blood,
redder than my cape
while the crowd, stunned,
rose to its feet and in one voice
shouted "Ole'!"

. . . .

. . . .

"Died in Amsterdam"
among the Van Goghs
without even cutting an ear.
Died of envy of the talent,
the pain, the genius,
the spark of insanity.
Died under a starry night,
among brilliant sunflowers,
calling out my brother's name
"Theo, Theo, where are you?"

"Died in Bali"
on the island of the turtle
died of enchantment, of ecstasy
during a trance dance
where the Gods,
chewing the beetlenut,
descended upon me
and showed me the magic mushroom
in their eyes so wise,
so wise, I cried and died
in Bali.

The church bell rings
way off in the distance
and the pealing echoes
through the countryside.
Women in the fields
raise their heads and listen.
The sound is grave
and full of foreboding.
There's death out there somewhere.
It stalks the farmhouse
and crawls into bed
with some unsuspecting soul.
She's a beautiful woman
whose breasts are firm
whose body is lithe
and whose loins beckon to be entered.
And she plays with him
and teases him
and makes him full of want.
And when he can stand it no more
he wraps his arms around her
as she wraps her legs around him
and fills him with bliss
till he's spent.
Then he lies there in her arms
as the death knell rings
way off in the distance
and the women in the fields
cross themselves
and bend to their task
to bring in the harvest
before winter comes.

There are trains
that can make you remember
and trains that can make you forget.
There are fast trains and freight trains,
and never get up late trains,
trains that hiss and screech to a halt
and trains that never stop.
There are trains that weave
in and out of crooked mountains,
over bridges, through tunnels,
and then stretch out for miles
on unending plains.
There are tunnels of the mind
where train whistles blow,
trains of thought
that go against the track
and pass our windows every day.
There are railroad crossings
where people wave
and others where people salute.
There are trains that belch out
smoke from the past,
iron horses
on which the fare is life itself.
There are trains that leave no tracks,
that crisscross each other
in geometric patterns,

. . . .

. . . .

in Picassos and Miros and Bracques.
There are trains that have no windows
and don't seem to be moving at all,
abandoned railroad cars
in railroad yards, at locks and crossings,
where the tracks are mined.
There are trains that can take you
to Auschwitz or Dachau or Treblinka.
There are trains in bombed out
railroad stations, waiting for passengers.
There are trains where hoboes
make their lives meaningful
by spending their time travelling.
There are trains that crash through our windows.

And then . . .
         . . . there is the last train.

Steal my thunder!
Break through to the core!
So many splinters under the skin.
Where do I go from here?

I hid five years
in the drawers of my life,
expecting to find them later on.
I was young and carefree
and it didn't matter.
Time was on my side.
There was shyness in laughter,
impatience with waiting,
and pimples of innocence on my face.
There was a pounding in my groin,
like the beat of my heart,
and a wanting I could not ignore.
And I reached for the sky,
and danced on my toes,
all in the space of the moment
between a single dawn
and the silvery twilight that follows.

So much time has gone by
since the swallows last flew south.
And those five years,
I cannot remember
in which closet I hid them.
And now that it matters
as never before,
I walk like a shadow
on broken bits of glass.

A nugget

When I was young
time was on my side.
There was shyness in laughter,
impatience with waiting,
and pimples of innocence on my face

I am not a river!
I do not flow on endlessly
to be cupped between two hands
at any point along the shore.
I am a fountain!
I stand in the square
in the middle of town
and only the thirsty
will reach for the cup
and only dry tongues
will water their palate.
But everyone has his own well now
and a pump that delivers
right to his house.
So the river flows on
though no one is thirsting
but the fountain stands idle
in the noonday sun.

A nugget

The river flows
where thirsty men
crouch down

I chisel away
on the stone tablets of time
scratching my words into essence
that others may breathe
the fragrance of flowers
I picked on my way to eternity.
For my eyes have seen the crocus
between the seasons of winter and spring
And I know that the stone
will soon turn to dust
and the words will return to their meaning.
A sword for a pen
a pen for a sword
the poet lays down with the warrior.
Everyone knows
a rose is a rose
but the end is ever so near
elusive, translucent
I hold in my hands
this thank you note to whoever

. . . .

. . . .

to heaven, to the stars,
to the dealer of cards,
to the Chef, the Mother,
the Great Weaver,
to Siddhartha, the ferry man,
to profound curiosity,
the unanswered question,
to the Bhagavad-Gita
and the Upanishads,
to the Prophet, the teacher,
the pain and the sorrow,
pathfinders all,
to the body that encased me
for performing so well,
to those who loved me
and those who didn't
for showing me my self
to the waters of the Ganges
and those of the Nile.
Let it all be etched in stone
that I have come this way
took water from this well
and moved out among the stars.

Light a fire
a funeral pyre
I do not bones allow.
The marrow bleeds
the good earth feeds
the cattle and the sow.
Rivulets
in sunken trenches
from my blistered soul
compost on the heap of time
where nothing else will grow.
Rice and wheat
and corn and barley
sprout from every field
where the dust of my body
was scattered and strewn,
a rich and bountiful yield.

Jay Frankston was raised in Paris, France, and came to the U.S. in 1942. He became a lawyer and practiced on his own in New York for nearly twenty years, reaching the top of his profession, sculpting and writing at the same time.

In 1972 he gave up law and New York and moved himself and his family to Northern California where he became a teacher and continued to sculpt and write.

He is the author of several books and of a true tale entitled "A Christmas Story", which was published in New York, condensed in *Reader's Digest*, and translated into 15 languages. He now lives in Little River, California, with his wife Monique.

WHOLE LOAF PUBLICATIONS
Little River, Ca. 95456
(707) 937-0208
e-mail wlp@mcn.org
http://www.mcn.org/a/wlp/christmas